SH*T MY BOSS SAYS

THE COLORING BOOK

AN INTERACTIVE, MARKET-PIONEERING, PARADIGM-SHIFTING, GAME-CHANGING COLORING BOOK

BY

PETRA MILTON

CONTAINS ADULT LANGUAGE

ISBN 978-1530566266

Three Ten Elk LLC

310elk.com

For more information contact hello@310elk.com.

INTRODUCTION

We all have them. Those erratic, egocentric, off-the-wall bosses. They tell you one thing and expect something different. They get involved in every minor detail and say they don't micromanage. They create approval processes and try to circumvent them. They constantly spew clichés, absurdities, and profanities.

We've been there. We've lived it. We've accepted it. We want to share these experiences and provide a way to channel all that angst, anxiety, and anger into a positive medium.

We created this coloring book because coloring has helped us get over the shit our bosses say. It's therapeutic and de-stressing. It's fun and creative. And best of all: it's quick and easy so we can get through a section during our lunch break.

We hope you enjoy all the quirky, cliché, funny, and bizarre types of shit your boss says. It was a blast to make.

Now go and color the shit out of these pages!

Share your shit with us and the world using #shitmybosssays

COLOR TEST PAGE

Try out your colored pencils,
pens, crayons, or whatever.

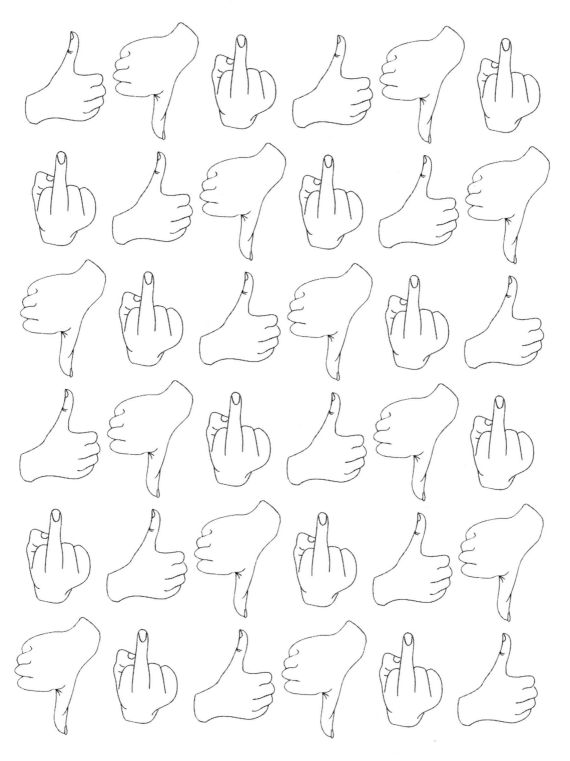

COLOR TEST PAGE

Try out your colored pencils,
pens, crayons, or whatever.

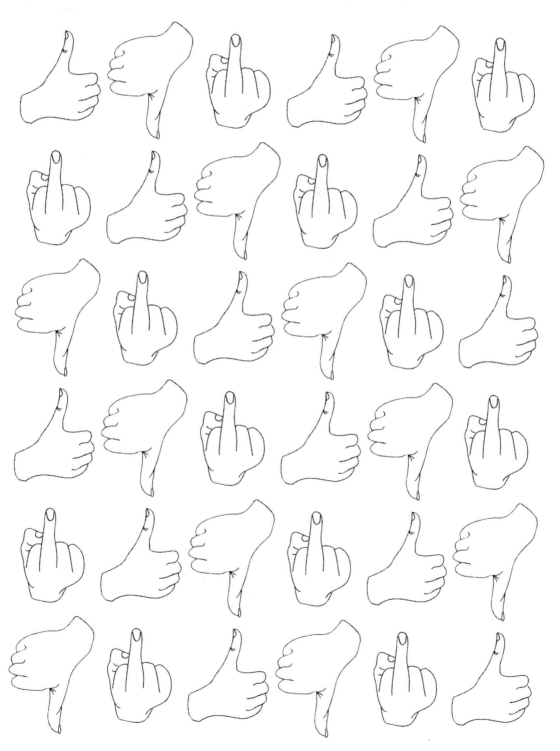

Don't bullshit a
BULLSHITTER,
I used to sell
used cars,

IDIOT. IT OBVIOUSLY FOLLOWS THE 80/20 RULE.

I'M IN THE MIDDLE OF SOMETHING. LET'S TALK AGAIN WHEN I HAVE FEWER BALLS.

I don't pay you
to think.

I would lose weight...
BUT I'M NOT A LOSER.

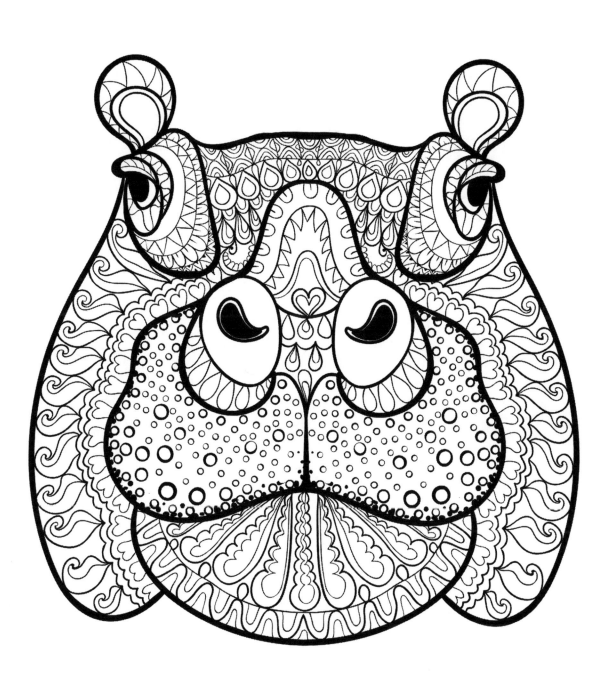

WELL, THAT'S SOME FUCKING HORSESHIT.

Pull your head out of your ASS.

THIS IS AMERICA,

I CAN DO WHATEVER I DAMN WELL PLEASE.

Irregardless, let's schedule time to CONVERSATE on over coffee.

I LOVE COFFEE

YOU HAVE TWO EARS AND ONE MOUTH FOR A REASON. SO SHUT THE FUCK UP AND LISTEN.

HOW DO YOU INTEND TO
FACE YOUR PROBLEM
IF YOUR PROBLEM IS YOUR

FACE.

You'll be a great fit here. Like a penguin in the desert.

GO AFTER THE LOW-HANGING FRUIT.

PRODUCT SAFETY ISSUES?

NOT A CHANCE!

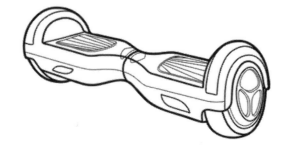

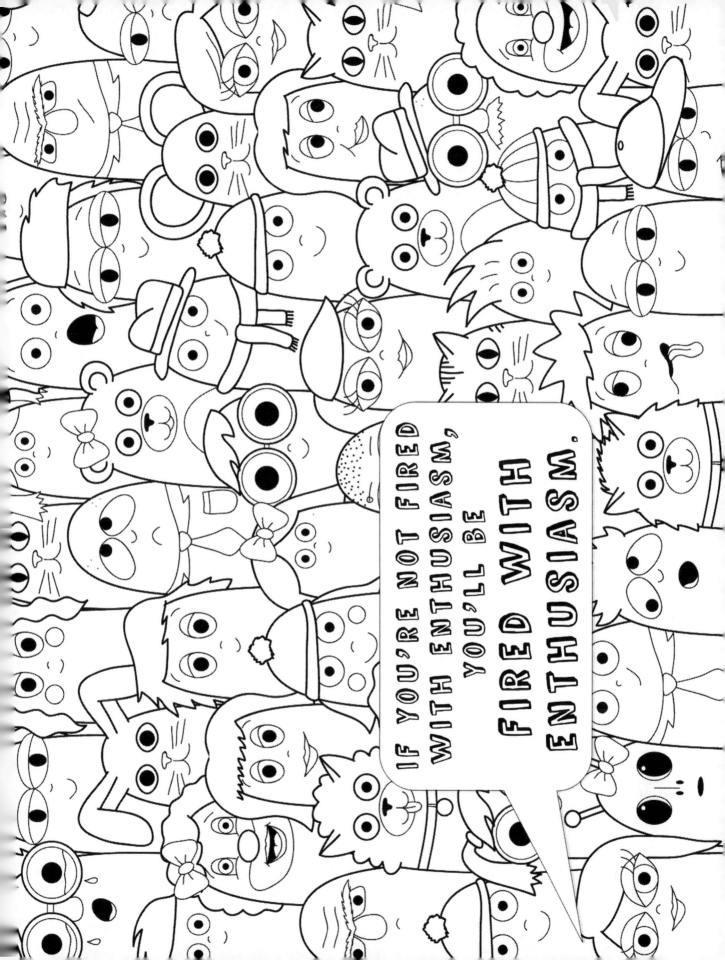

IF YOU
LISTEN
REALLY
CLOSELY,
YOU CAN
HEAR ME
NOT CARING.

WE HAVE AN UNLIMITED VACATION POLICY.

YOU CAN LEAVE AND NEVER COME BACK.

Made in the USA
San Bernardino, CA
21 November 2017